Supporting Phonics and Spelling

FOR AGES 7–8

Andrew Brodie

Contents

Andrew Brodie: Supporting Phonics & Spelling © A & C Black Publishers Ltd. 2006

Introduction

Supporting Phonics and Spelling is aimed at children in mainstream classrooms who have been identified as needing 'additional' or 'different' literacy support, particularly in phonics and spelling. The activities can be used by anyone working with children who fall into this category, whether you are a teacher, classroom assistant or parent.

Typically the seven to eight year-old children for whom the book is intended will be working at the levels expected of Year 1 or Year 2, or may simply need extra help in tackling the level of work appropriate for Year 3. Their difficulties may be short-term, and could be overcome with extra practice and support on a one-to-one or small group basis, or they may be long-term, where such support enables them to make progress but at a level behind their peer group. The activities in this book provide exactly what these children need – systematic repetition and practice of early phonic skills, based on a strong foundation of synthetic phonics and the best features of analytic phonics. The *Supporting Phonics and Spelling* series reflects the best practice in teaching spelling through phonics. It provides an approach that is:

- Systematic
- Multi-sensory
- Based on speaking and listening
- Linked closely to reading skills

This book is organised into three-page sets. It is vital that the teaching assistant or class teacher reads the 'Teacher's notes' on 'Sheet a' before starting the lesson. This first page in each set introduces specific phonemes and provides a good opportunity for the teacher and child to sound them out together. Children can also use their multi-sensory skills at this stage by drawing the letters in sand or making them out of dough or modelling clay. The second worksheet revises the same phonemes, but with a particular emphasis on speaking, listening and writing. The final worksheet in the set features a list of words containing the phonemes for further practice and consolidation. When used together, the three worksheets provide a thorough grounding in the phonic knowledge and skills that children need for confident reading, writing and spelling.

All the worksheets can be used on their own or alongside other literacy schemes that are already established within your school. The activities are simple and self-explanatory and the instruction text is deliberately kept to a minimum to make the pages easy to use for adults and less daunting for children to follow.

We recommend that the children use the *Supporting Phonics and Spelling* worksheets on a daily basis for approximately 20 minutes. Regular practice of previous learning is an integral part of the series. In completing the activities, teachers should place particular emphasis on speaking and listening skills.

Children generally achieve the greatest success in an atmosphere of support and encouragement. Praise from a caring adult can be the best reward for the children's efforts. The worksheets and activities in this book will provide many opportunities for children to enjoy these successes. The development of a positive attitude and the resulting increase in self-esteem will help them with all of their schoolwork.

Definitions and explanations of terms

(Please note that some publications will give slightly different definitions.)

Phoneme
A phoneme is a unit of sound and can be represented by:
one letter e.g. /b/ as in **b**at   two letters e.g. /ee/ as in sw**ee**t
three letters e.g. /ear/ as in n**ear**
Note that a phoneme can be represented in several different ways
e.g. the sound /ee/ can be represented by:

ee as in f**ee**t   **ei** as in c**ei**ling   **ie** as in ch**ie**f
ea as in n**ea**t   **i** as in sk**i**   **e_e** as in P**e**t**e**

Vowel phoneme
A vowel phoneme makes an open sound and always contains at least one vowel –
you usually have to open your mouth to say it.
Examples of vowel phonemes are:

/a/ as in b**a**t   /ie/ as in cr**ie**s   /oo/ as in b**oo**k
/ur/ as in t**ur**n   /ow/ as in t**ow**n

Consonant phoneme
A consonant phoneme always contains at least one consonant and usually involves
closing the mouth, 'biting' the lower lip, or touching the roof of the mouth with
the tongue. (There are exceptions e.g. /h/). Examples of consonant phonemes are:

/b/ as in **b**at   /f/ as in **ph**otograph
/th/ as in **th**ey   /ng/ as in si**ng**

Grapheme
A grapheme is a letter, a pair of letters or a group of letters representing a single
sound e.g. **ee**, **ei**, **ie**, **ea**, **i** and **e_e** are all graphemes representing the sound /ee/.

Grapheme/phoneme correspondence
The relationship between letters and the sounds that they represent.

Digraph
A digraph consists of two letters representing a single sound. So, for example, the
grapheme **ch** is a consonant digraph because it is made up of two consonants.
The grapheme **ee** is a vowel digraph and although it contains a consonant, **ow** is
also a vowel digraph, because it makes an open sound like a vowel does.

Split digraph
A split digraph consists of two vowels separated by a consonant to make one
phoneme e.g.   **e_e** as in P**e**t**e**   **i_e** as in m**i**n**e**   **a_e** as in c**a**m**e**

Trigraph
A trigraph is a group of three letters representing a single sound.
The vowel phonemes /air/ and /ear/ are trigraphs.

Cluster
A cluster consists of two or more letters making more than one sound. For example:
t   h   r   are three letters that can make the cluster **thr**, which
consists of the phonemes /th/ and /r/.

Blending
Blending is the process of combining different sounds (phonemes) to be able to say
a particular word or to make up part of a word e.g.
/sh/   /i/   /p/   can be blended to make the word ship.

/th/   /r/   are blended to make the cluster **thr**. Sometimes a cluster like this
will be called a blend.

Segmenting
Segmenting is the process of splitting a word into its different phonemes to be able
to spell it e.g. **ship** can be segmented into the three phonemes /sh/ /i/ /p/.

Onset and rime
The terms 'onset' and 'rime' are used together when analysing words. For example,
in the word 'cat' the phoneme represented by the letter 'c' is described as the onset
and the final cluster 'at' is described as the rime. Note that words that end with a
particular rime always rhyme but words that rhyme do not always contain the same
rime! For example, cat, rat and bat all end with the rime 'at' and all rhyme.
But the words tough and muff rhyme but have the rimes 'ough' and 'uff'.

vc
vowel/consonant e.g. the word *it*

cv
consonant/vowel e.g. the word *be*

cvc
consonant/vowel/consonant e.g. the word *cat*

ccvc
consonant/consonant/vowel/consonant e.g. the word *shop*

cvcc
consonant/vowel/consonant/consonant e.g. the word *fast*

Andrew Brodie: Supporting Phonics & Spelling © A & C Black Publishers Ltd. 2006

An introduction to phonemes

Language can be analysed by considering the separate sounds that combine to make up spoken words. These sounds are called phonemes and the English language has more than forty of them. It is possible to concentrate on forty-two main phonemes but here we list forty-four phonemes including those that are commonly used only in some regions of the country.

It is helpful to look at each phoneme individually and then at some sample words that demonstrate how the phoneme is represented by different graphemes as shown in the list below. Try reading each word out loud to spot the phoneme in each one. For the simple vowel sounds the graphemes are shown in bold text.

Vowel phonemes	Sample words
/a/	b**a**t
/e/	l**e**g, g**ue**ss, h**ea**d, s**ai**d, s**ay**s
/i/	b**i**g, plant**e**d, b**u**sy, cr**y**stal, d**e**cide, **e**xact, g**u**ilt, r**e**peat
/o/	d**o**g, **ho**nest, w**a**s, qu**a**rrel, tr**ou**gh, v**au**lt, y**ach**t (the ch is silent)
/u/	b**u**g, l**o**ve, bl**oo**d, c**o**mfort, r**ou**gh, y**ou**ng
/ae/	rain, day, game, navy, weigh, they, great, rein
/ee/	been, team, field, these, he, key, litre, quay, suite
/ie/	pie, high, sign, my, bite, child, guide, guy, haiku
/oe/	boat, goes, crow, cone, gold, sew
/ue/	soon, do, July, blue, chew, June, bruise, shoe, you, move, through
/oo/	book, put
/ar/	barn, bath (regional), laugh (regional), baa, half, clerk, heart, guard
/ur/	Thursday, girl, her, learn, word
/or/	born, door, warm, all, draw, cause, talk, aboard, abroad, before, four, bought, taught
/ow/	brown, found, plough
/oi/	join, toy, buoy
/air/	chair, pear, care, where, their, prayer
/ear/	near, cheer, here, weird, pier

Try saying this vowel phoneme in the sample words:

/er/	fast**er**, g**a**zump, curr**a**nt, wooll**e**n, circ**us**

Not to be confused with the phoneme /ur/, this phoneme is very similar to /u/ but is slightly different in some regions.

Consonant phonemes with sample words

/b/	bag, rub
/d/	dad, could
/f/	off, calf, fast, graph, tough
/g/	ghost, girl, bag
/h/	here, who
/j/	bridge, giraffe, huge, jet
/k/	kite, antique, cat, look, quiet, choir, sock, six (note that the sound made by the letter x is a blend of the phonemes /k/ and /s/)
/l/	leg, crawl, full
/m/	mug, climb, autumn
/n/	now, gnash, knight, sign, fun
/p/	peg, tap
/r/	run, wrote
/s/	cinema, goose, listen, psalm, scene, see, sword, yes, less
/t/	ten, sit, receipt
/v/	vest, love
/w/	wet
/wh/	when (regional)
/y/	yes
/z/	choose, was, zoo
/th/	the, with
/th/	thank, path
/ch/	cheer, such, match
/sh/	shop, rush, session, chute
/zh/	usual
/ng/	thing, think

For some phonemes you may dispute some of the examples that we have listed. This may be due to regional variations in pronunciation. Disputing the sounds is a positive step as it ensures that you are analysing them!

It is not necessary to teach the children all the graphemes for each phoneme but to be ready and aware when pupils suggest words to you to represent a particular sound. They are not wrong with their suggestions and should be praised for recognising the phoneme. You can then show them how the words that they have suggested are written but that normally the particular sound is represented by a specific grapheme.

Examining the list of high frequency words

These words from the high frequency list for Years 1 and 2 do not always follow simple phonic patterns, although all of them include phonic elements that follow a typical pattern. Children will find them easier to tackle through developing the phonic skills that we are encouraging in this series of books: listening to sounds, speaking the sounds clearly and segmenting words into sounds that can be matched to appropriate letters, ie matching phonemes to appropriate graphemes.

about	could	his	name	red	took
after	did	home	new	saw	twelve
again	dig	house	next	school	twenty
an	do	how	night	seen	two
another	don't	if	nine	should	us
as	door	jump	not	sister	very
back	down	just	now	so	want
ball	first	last	off	some	way
be	from	laugh	old	take	were
because	girl	little	once	ten	what
bed	good	lived	one	than	when
been	got	love	or	that	where
blue	had	made	our	their	who
boy	half	make	out	them	will
brother	has	man	over	then	with
but	have	many	people	there	would
by	help	may	pull	these	your
called	her	more	push	three	
came	here	much	put	time	
can't	him	must	ran	too	

Some of these words are included in the phonic lists in this book and some are included as 'odd ones out'. You may like to introduce other words from the list as opportunities arise, supporting the children in segmenting the words to be able to spell them. Below is the list of focus words that appear in this book, though many others are included within the activities.

after	drain	grin	old	skin	tea
again	dream	grip	one	skip	team
ball	dress	grit	pie	sky	three
boat	drill	groan	pies	slam	tie
boot	drop	hall	plain	sleep	ties
bump	drum	have	pram	slid	time
call	dry	house	pray	slide	toad
camp	east	huff	press	slop	too
chain	eat	hump	price	slope	track
cheek	fall	igloo	print	slug	train
child	flag	jump	prize	small	trap
cliff	flake	lamp	prod	sniff	tray
coat	flash	leaf	rain	Spain	tree
cold	flashing	lie	road	spoon	trick
could	float	like	said	stall	truck
crab	fluff	limp	saw	stamp	try
crash	fly	load	school	stand	wall
cream	flying	magpie	sea	star	week
cried	from	main	sheep	start	wild
cries	girl	make	shoot	stay	would
cross	goat	meal	should	stiff	you
crust	gold	moon	skate	sting	your
cry	gram	name	skid	stuck	zoo
damp	grand	new	skill	stuff	
door	green	off	skim	sweep	

Andrew Brodie: Supporting Phonics & Spelling © A & C Black Publishers Ltd. 2006

1a

Learning objective

Phonemes
Consonants: /b/,/k/,/d/,/j/,/l/,/p/,/m/,/h/
Vowels: /a/,/i/,/u/

Target words
camp, damp, lamp, jump, bump, hump, limp, have

Teacher's notes

Worksheet 1a

- Photocopy this page and help the child to cut out the letter tiles.

- Revise the phonemes (sounds) with the child. Depending on your school's policy you may wish to encourage the child to repeat both the names of the letters and the sounds they make in each of the words (*camp, damp, lamp, jump, bump, hump, limp, have*).

- In most of the words in this set the phonemes /m/ and /p/ are blended together, although they are two distinct sounds. Discuss the two letters and the sounds that they make individually, then help the child say the consonant cluster **mp** – the way the **m** sounds is quite different from the way it sounds in isolation.

- When you feel the child is confident with the phonemes, help him/her to blend the sounds and arrange the letter tiles to make words. There are many words that can be made, including for example *plum* and *map*. Praise the child for finding these but then encourage him/her to experiment with words that end with the consonant cluster **mp**. In addition to the target words the child may find others: *lump* and *dump* for example.

Worksheet 1b

- Ask the child to point to the letters at the top of the page and to tell you the sounds they make.

- Dictate the words **camp, damp, lamp, jump, bump, hump, limp, have** one at a time. You may need to repeat each word several times to help the child segment it into phonemes so that s/he can write it.

- As an additional activity you could make up some oral sentences together using some of the words and pointing at these words as you say them e.g. *A camel may have one hump or two. It was damp at the camp.*

- Write down one of the sentences for the child to copy. Encourage him/her to write clearly, following the school's handwriting policy for letter formation, and to start the sentence with a capital letter and to end it with a full stop.

Worksheet 1c

- This sheet includes the seven target words with the cluster **mp** at the end of each one together with an extra word, *have*. The extra word is a useful high frequency word and can be used for an 'odd one out' activity.

- This sheet could be copied for display purposes but can also be used to provide extra practice in writing the words. There are three writing lines for each word, enabling the child to use large and smaller writing. You could write each word on the first of the two smaller writing lines so that the child can copy your writing in the correct style used by your school.

LETTER TILES

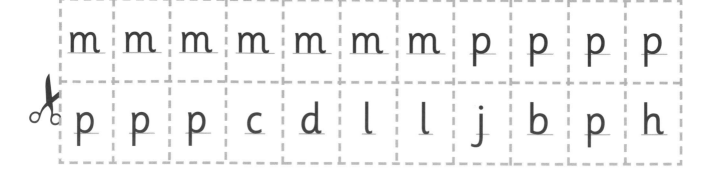

Andrew Brodie: Supporting Phonics & Spelling © A & C Black Publishers Ltd. 2006

What sounds do the letters make?

m p c d l j b p h

Listen to your teacher. Write the words.

_____   _____

_____   _____

_____   _____

Write a sentence using one or more of the words.

_____

_____

_____

Name: **Date:**

Words for today

camp

damp

lamp

jump

bump

hump

limp

have

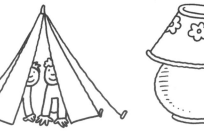    

Learning objective

Phonemes
Consonants: /ch/,/k/ (as grapheme c),
/d/ (as graphemes d and ld), /l/,/w/,/sh/,/g/
Vowels: /oe/ (as grapheme o), /ie/ (as grapheme i),
/u/ (as grapheme ou)

Target words
old, cold, gold, child,
wild, could, would,
should

Teacher's notes

Worksheet 2a

- Photocopy this page and help the child to cut out the target words.

- Help the child blend the phonemes to read the words, taking the opportunity to revise the phonemes. Depending on your school's policy you may wish to encourage the child to repeat both the names of the letters and the sounds they make in each of the words (*old, cold, gold, child, wild, could, would, should*).

Worksheet 2b

- Discuss the sounds made by the letters at the top of the page, concentrating first on the consonant phonemes /k/, /d/, /l/, /w/, /g/, /sh/, /ch/ then the blend **ld**.

- Now look at the letters **o** and **i**. Discuss the fact that these letters sometimes say /o/ and /i/ but in today's words they are saying their own names /oe/ and /ie/.

- Dictate the words **old, cold, gold, child**, **wild** to the child, supporting him/her in segmenting each word into its phonemes, so that s/he can choose the correct letters to spell each word. You may need to repeat each word several times, making sure that the phonemes are pronounced clearly.

- Now dictate the sentences below, repeating them regularly and providing lots of time for the child to write them. Encourage him/her to write clearly, following the school's handwriting policy for letter formation, and to start the sentence with a capital letter and to end it with a full stop. The child may need to see some of the words, such as *said*, so if appropriate you could show the child each complete sentence before you dictate it. The sentences are:

  The old man said that the child was wild.
  The old ring was made of gold.
  The sun was out but it was a cold day.

Worksheet 2c

- This sheet includes the five target words with the consonant cluster **ld** at the end of each one together with three extra words, *could, would* and *should*. The extra words are useful high frequency words and can be used to demonstrate exceptions, including the existence of 'silent' letters (in these words there is a silent **l**). Help the child to recognise the fact that the letters **o** and **u** together are saying /oo/ (like book) in these words.

- This sheet could be copied for display purposes but can also be used to provide the child with extra practice in writing the words.

- There are three writing lines for each word, enabling the child to use large and smaller writing. You could write each word on the first of the two smaller writing lines so that the child can copy your writing in the correct style used by your school.

TARGET WORDS

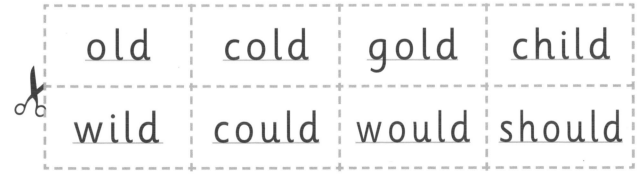

| old | cold | gold | child |
| wild | could | would | should |

Name: **Date:**

What sounds do the letters make?

c d l w g sh ch ld o i

Listen to your teacher. Write the words.

_____ _____ _____ _____

Listen to your teacher. Write the sentences.

_____

_____

_____

_____

_____

_____

_____

Name: **Date:**

Words for today

old

cold

gold

child

wild

could

would

should

Learning objective

| **Phonemes**
Consonants: /f/,/l/,/m/,/s/,/t/
Vowels: /a/,/ee/ (as grapheme ea), /er/ | **Target words**
eat, east, leaf, meal, sea, tea, team, after |

Teacher's notes

Worksheet 3a

- Photocopy this page and then help the child to cut out the target words.

- Help the child blend the phonemes to read the words, taking the opportunity to revise the phonemes. Depending on your school's policy you may wish to encourage the child to repeat both the names of the letters and the sounds they make in each of the words (*eat, east, leaf, meal, sea, tea, team, after*).

Worksheet 3b

- Ask the child to point to the letters at the top of the page and to tell you the sounds they make.

- Dictate the words **eat, east, leaf, meal, sea, tea, team, after** to the child, supporting him/her in segmenting each word into its phonemes so that s/he can write it. You may need to repeat each word several times, making sure that the phonemes are pronounced clearly. Showing the target words to the child and then covering them while you dictate the words can be a very effective technique. It is important that the child is fully supported and gains lots of praise where s/he is successful, even with part of a word.

- Ensure that the child has seen each word correctly written before asking him/her to attempt to write the words in the appropriate places in the sentences. The sentences include quite complex words and the child might need some help in reading them. Encourage the child to make sense of the sentences so that the task of inserting words is made easier.

- As an additional activity you could make up some extra sentences together using some of the words and pointing at the target words on the sheet as you say them e.g. *After my meal I have a cup of tea. I do like to be beside the sea.*

- You could write down one of the sentences for the child to copy. Encourage him/her to write clearly, following the school's handwriting policy for letter formation, and to start the sentence with a capital letter and to end it with a full stop.

Worksheet 3c

- This sheet includes the seven target words with the grapheme **ea** in each one together with an extra word, *after*. The extra word is a useful high frequency word and can be used for an 'odd one out' activity.

- This sheet can be copied for display purposes but can also be used to provide the child with extra practice in writing the words. There are three writing lines for each word, enabling the child to use large and smaller writing. You could write each word on the first of the two smaller writing lines so that s/he can copy your writing in the correct style used by your school.

TARGET WORDS

| eat | east | leaf | meal |
| sea | tea | team | after |

Name: **Date:**

What sounds do the letters make?

f   l   m   s   t   a   er   ea

Listen to your teacher. Write the words.

_____   _____

_____   _____

_____   _____

_____   _____

Use the correct words to fill the
gaps in these sentences.

A_____ fell off the tree.

The county of Norfolk is on
the _____ side of England.

The _____ played
really well yesterday.

Now write a sentence of your own.

_____

_____

Name:

Date:

Words for today

eat

east

leaf

meal

sea

tea

team

after

4a

Learning objective

Phonemes
Consonants: /r/,/m/,/p/,/ch/,/s/,/t/,/n/,/g/,/d/
Vowels: /ae/,/a/,/or/

Target words
rain, main, plain, chain,
Spain, train, again, door

Teacher's notes

Worksheet 4a

- Photocopy this page and help the child to cut out the target words.

- Help the child blend the phonemes to read the words, taking the opportunity to revise the phonemes. Depending on your school's policy you may wish to encourage the child to repeat both the names of the letters and the sounds they make in each of the words (*rain, main, plain, chain, Spain, train, again, door*).

- Point out that the word *again* is a two syllable word and discuss the sound that **ai** makes in this word. Is it the same sound as in the word *rain*? In some regions of the country the **ai** grapheme in *again* will make the phoneme /ae/ as in the word *rain* whereas in other regions the **ai** grapheme will make the phoneme /e/.

Worksheet 4b

- Ask the child to point to the letters at the top of the page and to tell you the sounds they make.

- Dictate the following sentences to the child:

  The train is going to Spain.
  The main door is locked with a chain.
  It is going to rain again.

- Support the child in writing the dictated sentences by helping him/her to segment each word into phonemes. Encourage him/her to write clearly, following the school's handwriting policy for letter formation, and to start each sentence with a capital letter and to end it with a full stop.

Worksheet 4c

- This sheet includes the seven target words with the grapheme **ai** in each one together with an extra word, *door*. The extra word is a useful high frequency word and can be used for an 'odd one out' activity.

- This sheet can be copied for display purposes but can also be used to provide the child with extra practice in writing the words. There are three writing lines for each word, enabling the child to use large and smaller writing. You could write each word on the first of the two smaller writing lines so that the child can copy your writing in the correct style used by your school.

TARGET WORDS

| rain | main | plain | chain |
| Spain | train | again | door |

Name: **Date:**

What sounds do the letters make?

r m p s t n g d ch ai a

Listen to your teacher. Write the sentences.

Spain

Name: _____ **Date:** _____

Words for today

rain _____ _____

main _____ _____

plain _____ _____

chain _____ _____

Spain _____ _____

train _____ _____

again _____ _____

door _____

Spain

5a

Phonemes
Consonants: /l/,/p/,/t/,/k/ (as grapheme c), /r/, /z/ (as grapheme s), /m/,/g/,/f/
Vowels: /ie/,/a/,/o/

Target words
lie, tie, ties, pie, pies, cried, magpie, from

Teacher's notes

Worksheet 5a

- Photocopy this sheet and help the child to cut out the target words.

- Help the child blend the phonemes to read the words, taking the opportunity to revise the phonemes. Depending on your school's policy you may wish to encourage the child to repeat both the names of the letters and the sounds they make in each of the words (*lie, tie, ties, pie, pies, cried, magpie, from*).

- In all the words in this set, apart from the odd-one-out word, the letters **i** and **e** together form the phoneme /ie/. Discuss the two letters and help the child to say the phoneme /ie/.

- On these pages the 'odd one out' high frequency word is *from*. Draw the child's attention to this word and encourage him/her to understand the importance of spelling it correctly each time it is used in their writing.

Worksheet 5b

- Ask the child to point to the letters at the top of the page and to tell you the sounds they make.

- Help the child read the sentence to decide which two words fit into the spaces. According to the ability of each child, you may ask the child to either stick the words into the correct positions by the pictures or write the words themselves using their target words as a guide. This section of the activity provides the opportunity to talk about adding **s** to some words to create plurals.

- As an additional activity you could make up some extra sentences together using some of the words and pointing at the target words on the sheet as you say them e.g. *I got a pie from the shop. I can put on my tie.*

- You could write one of the sentences for the child to copy, or dictate the sentence for the child to try to write by segmenting the words into their phonemes. If you do the latter it is important to use words that are simple to write and to praise the child for all reasonable attempts at completing this task. Encourage him/her to write clearly, following the school's handwriting policy for letter formation, and to start the sentence with a capital letter and to end it with a full stop.

Worksheet 5c

- This sheet includes the seven target words with the phoneme /ie/, together with the extra word, *from*.

- This sheet could be copied for display purposes but can also be used to provide the child with extra practice in writing the words. There are three writing lines for each word, enabling the child to use large and smaller writing. You may like to write each word on the first of the two smaller writing lines so that the child can copy your writing in the correct style used by your school.

TARGET WORDS

| lie | pie | pies | tie |
| ties | cried | magpie | from |

Name: _____ **Date:** _____

What sounds do the letters make?

l p t c r s m g f ie a o

Stick or write the correct words in the spaces in the sentence.

"I will not tell a_____",
                    the girl from my class.

Stick the correct words by the pictures.

_____   _____   _____

_____   _____

Name: _____ **Date:** _____

Words for today

lie _____ _____

tie _____ _____

ties _____ _____

pie _____ _____

pies _____ _____

cried _____ _____

magpie _____ _____

from _____ _____

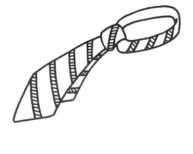

Andrew Brodie: Supporting Phonics & Spelling © A & C Black Publishers Ltd. 2006

Learning objective

6a

Phonemes
Consonants: /b/,/k/ (as grapheme c), /t/,/f/, /l/,/r/,/d/,/s/,/g/

Vowels: /oe/ (as grapheme oa), /e/ (as grapheme ai)

Target words
boat, coat, goat, float, load, toad, road, said

Teacher's notes

Worksheet 6a

- Photocopy this sheet and help the child to cut out the target words.

- Seven of the words in this set contain the grapheme **oa**. Discuss the two letters and the sounds they make individually and then help the child to say the phoneme /oe/. Help the child blend the phonemes to read the words, taking the opportunity to revise the phonemes. Depending on your school's policy you may wish to encourage the child to repeat both the names of the letters and the sounds they make in each of the words (*boat, coat, goat, float, load, toad, road, said*).

- On these pages the 'odd one out' high frequency word is *said*. Draw the child's attention to this word and encourage him/her to understand the importance of spelling it correctly each time it is used in their writing.

Worksheet 6b

- Ask the child to point to the letters and the top of the page and to tell you the sounds they make.

- Help the child to decide where each word should be used to label the picture. According to the ability of each child you may ask him/her to either stick the words into the correct positions or write the words themselves, using their cut-out words as a guide. The children will not need all of the words when labelling the picture.

- As an additional activity you could make up some extra sentences together using some of the words and pointing at the target words on the sheet as you say them e.g. *"I can float,"* said the goat. Load up the boat.*

- You could write one of the sentences for the child to copy or you could dictate the sentence for the child to try to write. If you do the latter it is important to use words that are simple to write and to praise the child for all reasonable attempts at completing this task. Encourage him/her to write clearly, following the school's handwriting policy for letter formation, and to start the sentence with a capital letter and to end it with a full stop.

Worksheet 6c

- This sheet includes the seven target words with the grapheme **oa**, together with the extra word, *said*.

- This sheet could be copied for display purposes but can also be used to provide the child with extra practice in writing the words. There are three writing lines for each word, enabling the child to use large and smaller writing. You could write each word on the first of the two smaller writing lines so that the child can copy your writing in the correct style used by your school.

TARGET WORDS

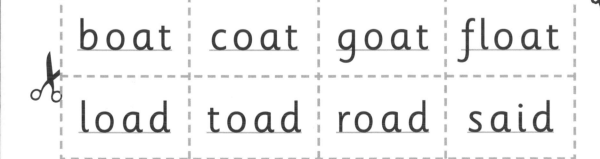

| boat | coat | goat | float |
| load | toad | road | said |

6b **Name:** **Date:**

What sounds do the letters make?

b   c   t   g   f   l   r   s   oa

Use the words to help you label the picture.

24   Andrew Brodie: Supporting Phonics & Spelling   © A & C Black Publishers Ltd. 2006

Name: _____   **Date:** _____

Words for today

boat _____   _____

coat _____   _____

goat _____   _____

float _____   _____

load _____   _____

toad _____   _____

road _____   _____

said _____   _____

Learning objective

Phonemes
Consonants: /b/,/t/,/m/,/n/,/s/,/p/,/g/,/l/,/z/, /sh/,/h/
Vowels: /ue/ (as grapheme oo), /i/,/ow/ (as grapheme ou)

Target words
boot, too, moon, spoon, igloo, zoo, shoot, house

Teacher's notes

Worksheet 7a

- Photocopy this sheet and help the child to cut out the letter tiles.

- Revise the phonemes with the child. Depending on your school's policy you may wish to encourage the child to repeat both the names of the letters and the sounds they make in each of the words (*boot, too, moon, spoon, igloo, zoo, shoot, house*). In this set of words the digraph **oo** forms the phoneme /ue/.

Worksheet 7b

- Read each of the words **boot, too, moon, spoon, igloo, zoo, shoot, house** to the child and help him/her to select the correct letters to fill the spaces.

- Encourage him/her to read each word aloud, blending the phonemes where necessary to read the more difficult words. The 'odd one out' high frequency word is *house*. Draw the child's attention to this word and encourage him/her to understand the importance of spelling it correctly each time it is used in their writing.

- Next the child should read the sentence and draw a picture to go with it.

- As an additional activity you could make up some extra sentences together using some of the words and pointing at the target words on the sheet as you say them e.g. *I eat with a spoon. My house is not an igloo.*

- You could write one of the sentences for the child to copy, or dictate a sentence for the child to try to write. If you do the latter it is important to use words that are simple to write and to praise the child for all reasonable attempts at completing this task. Encourage him/her to write clearly, following the school's handwriting policy for letter formation, and to start the sentence with a capital letter and to end it with a full stop.

Worksheet 7c

- This sheet includes the seven target words with the grapheme **oo**, together with the extra word, *house*. This sheet can be copied for display purposes but could also be used to provide the child with extra practice in writing the words. There are three writing lines for each word, enabling the child to use large and smaller writing. You could write each word on the first of the two smaller writing lines so that the child can copy your writing in the correct style used by your school.

LETTER TILES

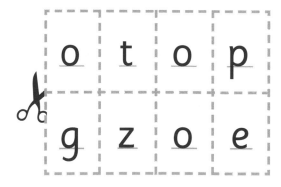

Listen to your teacher.
Use the letter tiles to complete the words.

b ___ o t   ___ oo   m ___ on

s ___ oon   i ___ loo   ___ oo

sho ___ t   hous ___

Read the sentence. Draw a picture to go with the sentence.

I can see the igloo in the zoo.

Now copy the sentence.

_____

_____

Name: _____ **Date:** _____

Words for today

boot _____ _____

too _____ _____

moon _____ _____

spoon _____ _____

igloo _____ _____

zoo _____ _____

shoot _____ _____

house _____ _____

Learning objective

Phonemes	**Target words**
Consonants: /k/ (as grapheme c), /r/,/b/, /z/ (as grapheme s), s/,/t/,/sh/,/m/,/k/,/l/ **Vowels:** /ee/ (as grapheme ea), /a/,/o/,/ie/	crab, cry, cries, crust, crash, cream, cross, like

Teacher's notes

Worksheet 8a

- Photocopy this sheet and help the child to cut out the letter tiles.

- Depending on your school's policy you may wish to encourage the child to repeat both the names of the letters and the sounds they make in each of the words (*crab, cry, cries, crust, crash, cream, cross, like*). In this set of words the grapheme **cr** appears at the beginning of each one. Discuss the letters and the sound they make individually then support the child in saying the cluster **cr**.

- On these pages the 'odd one out', high frequency word is *like*. There should be a close focus on this word and children should be encouraged to understand the importance of being in the good habit of spelling it correctly each time it is used in their writing.

Worksheet 8b

- Read each of the words to the child and help him/her select the correct letter/s to fill each space. Encourage him/her to read each word aloud, blending the phonemes where necessary to read the more difficult words.

- The child can then draw lines to match the words to the five small pictures.

- As an additional activity you could make up some extra sentences together using some of the words and pointing at the target words on the sheet as you say them e.g. *I cry when I am cross. My dad likes to eat crab with cream.*

- You could write one of the sentences for the child to copy, or dictate a sentence for the child to try to write. If you do the latter it is important to use words that are simple to write and to praise the child for all reasonable attempts at completing this task. Encourage him/her to write clearly, following the school's handwriting policy for letter formation, and to start the sentence with a capital letter and to end it with a full stop.

Worksheet 8c

- This sheet includes the seven target words with the cluster **cr**, together with the extra word, *like*. This sheet can be copied for display purposes but could also be used to provide the child with extra practice in writing the words. There are three writing lines for each word, enabling the child to use large and smaller writing. You may like to write each word on the first of the two smaller writing lines so that the child can copy your writing in the correct style used by your school.

LETTER TILES

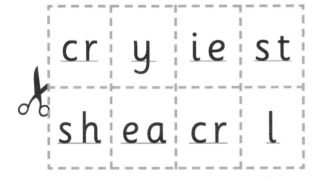

Name: **Date:**

Listen to your teacher.
Use the letter tiles to complete the words.

___ a b   cr ___   cr ___ s

cru ___   cra ___   cr ___ m

___ oss    ___ ike

Now write the words.

crab _____

crust _____

cross _____

crash _____

Andrew Brodie: Supporting Phonics & Spelling © A & C Black Publishers Ltd. 2006

Name: _____   **Date:** _____

Words for today

crab   _____   _____

cry   _____   _____

cries   _____   _____

crust   _____   _____

crash   _____   _____

cream   _____   _____

cross   _____   _____

like   _____   _____

Learning objective

Phonemes
Consonants: /s/,/l/,/m/,/p/,/d/,/g/,
/k/ (as grapheme ch)
Vowels: /ue/ (as grapheme oo), /ee/,/i/,/u/,/ie/,/oe/

Target words
slam, sleep, slug, slid,
slide, slop, slope, school

Teacher's notes

Worksheet 9a

- Photocopy this page and help the child to cut out the target words.

- Help the child blend the phonemes to read the words, taking the opportunity to revise the phonemes. Depending on your school's policy you may wish to encourage the child to repeat both the names of the letters and the sounds they make in each of the words (*slam, sleep, slug, slid, slide, slop, slope, school*).

- Look in particular at the consonants **s** and **l** and how they blend together in the cluster **sl**. Explain that seven of the words begin with **sl**, then focus on the vowel digraphs in the words *slope* and *slide*, explaining that the final **e** changes the sound of the preceding vowel e.g. the final **e** in the word *slope* changes the vowel **o** from the phoneme /o/ to the phoneme /oe/.

- Look too at the spelling of the 'odd one out' word *school*.

Worksheet 9b

- Ask the child to point to the letters at the top of the page and to tell you the sounds they make.

- Dictate the words **slam, sleep, slug, slid, slide, slop, slope, school** to the child, helping him/her to segment each word into its phonemes so that s/he can choose the correct letters to spell the word.

- Now dictate the sentences below, repeating them regularly and providing lots of time for the child to write them. Encourage him/her to write clearly, following the school's handwriting policy for letter formation, and to start the sentence with a capital letter and end it with a full stop. Some children may need to see some of the words. You could show the child each complete sentence before you dictate it. The sentences are:

A slim slug went to sleep on a slope.
The boy slid down a slide at school.
Can you slam the door?

Worksheet 9c

- This sheet includes the seven target words with the consonant cluster **sl**, together with the extra word *school*. The extra word is a useful high frequency word. It is important to focus on the spelling of the word *school*, particularly the way the **sch** sounds like **sk**.

- This sheet can be copied for display purposes but can also be used to provide the child with extra practice in writing the words. There are three lines for each word enabling the child to use large and smaller writing. You may like to write each word on the first of the two smaller lines so that the child can copy your writing in the correct style used by your school.

TARGET WORDS

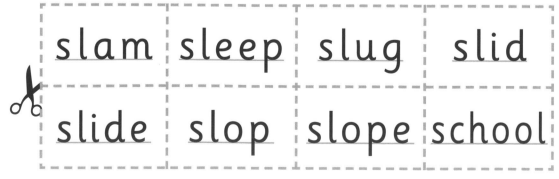

| slam | sleep | slug | slid |
| slide | slop | slope | school |

Andrew Brodie: Supporting Phonics & Spelling © A & C Black Publishers Ltd. 2006

Name: **Date:**

What sounds do the letters make?

sl   ee   u   i   m   d   a

Listen to your teacher. Write the words.

_____   _____   _____   _____

_____   _____   _____   _____

Listen to your teacher. Write the sentences.

Name: **Date:**

Words for today

slam

sleep

slug

slid

slide

slop

slope

school

10a

Learning objective	
Phonemes **Consonants:** /g/,/r/,/n/,/p/,/t/,/m/,/d/ **Vowels:** /i/,/oe/ (as grapheme oa), /a/, /ee/,/ae/ (as split digraph a_e)	**Target words** grin, grip, grit, groan, gram, grand, green, name

Teacher's notes

Worksheet 10a

- Photocopy this page and help the child to cut out the target words.
- Help the child blend the phonemes to read the words, taking the opportunity to revise the phonemes. Depending on your school's policy you may wish to encourage the child to repeat both the names of the letters and the sounds they make in each of the words (*grin, grip, grit, groan, gram, grand, green, name*).
- In this set of words, the consonant cluster **gr** appears at the beginning of each one, except for the 'odd one out' word, *name*. Discuss the two letters and the sounds they make individually then help the child to say the cluster **gr**.
- On these pages the 'odd one out' high frequency word is *name*. There should be a close focus on this word and children should be encouraged to understand the importance of getting into the habit of spelling it correctly each time it is used in their writing.

Worksheet 10b

- Help the child to select the correct words to complete the sentences. You could encourage the child to stick the target words in the correct spaces, or you may decide to ask the child to write each word by segmenting the word into its phonemes. The child will not need to use all the given words to complete the sentences.
- As an additional activity you could make up some extra sentences together using some of the words and pointing at the target words on the sheet as you say them e.g. *My gran is green and very grand*.
- Write down one of the sentences for the child to copy, or dictate the sentence for the child to try to write. If you do the latter it is important to use words that are simple to write and to praise the child for all reasonable attempts at completing this task. Encourage him/her to write clearly, following the school's handwriting policy for letter formation, and to start the sentence with a capital letter and to end it with a full stop.

Worksheet 10c

- This sheet includes the seven target words beginning with the letters **gr**, together with an extra word, *name*.
- This sheet could be copied for display purposes but can also be used to provide the child with extra practice in writing the words. There are three writing lines for each word, enabling the child to use large and smaller writing. You may like to write each word on the first of the two smaller writing lines so that the child can copy your writing in the correct style used by your school.

TARGET WORDS

grin	grip	grit	groan
gram	grand	green	name

Read the words you have cut out.
Read the sentences. Put the missing words into the sentences. Copy each sentence.

There is _____ grass
in the field.

_____

_____

He gave a _____ when
he was hurt.

_____

_____

I _____ when I am happy.

_____

_____

The girl got some _____
in her eyes.

_____

_____

Name: _____   **Date:** _____

Words for today

grin _____ _____

grip _____ _____

grit _____ _____

groan _____ _____

gram _____ _____

grand _____ _____

green _____ _____

name _____ _____

Learning objective

Phonemes
Consonants: /f/,/l/,/g/,/k/,/sh/,/ng/,/y/
Vowels: /a/,/ai/ (as split digraph a_e),
/oe/ (as in grapheme oa), /ue/ (as grapheme ou), /i/,
/ie/ (as grapheme y)

Target words
flag, flake, flash,
float, fly, flying,
flashing, you

Teacher's notes

Worksheet 11a

- Photocopy this page and help the child to cut out the target words.

- Help the child blend the phonemes to read the words, taking the opportunity to revise the phonemes. Depending on your school's policy you may wish to encourage the child to repeat both the names of the letters and the sounds they make in each of the words (*flag, flake, flash, float, fly, flying, flashing, you*).

- Point out that the words flying and flashing are two syllable words, both ending with **ing**. Can the child describe the two sounds that make up **ing**: /i/ and /ng/? This is part of the segmenting process that is necessary to spell the words

Worksheet 11b

- Dictate the following sentences to the child, providing support with words such as *pole* and *light* that are not in the list of target words, by encouraging the child to segment the words into their phonemes:

  The flag is flying on the flag pole.
  Can you fly or can you float?
  There is a light flashing in the sky.

- As an additional activity you could make up some oral sentences together using some of the words and pointing at the target words on the sheet as you say them. Write down one of the sentences for the child to copy. Encourage him/her to write clearly, following the school's handwriting policy for letter formation, and to start each sentence with a capital letter and to end it with a full stop.

Worksheet 11c

- This sheet includes the seven target words with the consonant cluster **fl** in each one together with an extra word, *you*. The extra word is a useful high frequency word and can be used for an 'odd one out' activity.

- This sheet could be copied for display purposes but can also be used to provide the child with extra practice in writing the words. There are three writing lines for each word, enabling the child to use large and smaller writing. You may like to write each word on the first of the two smaller writing lines so that the child can copy your writing in the correct style used by your school.

TARGET WORDS

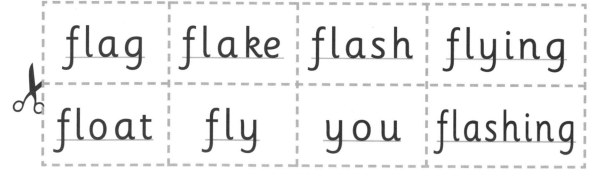

Listen to your teacher. Write the sentences.

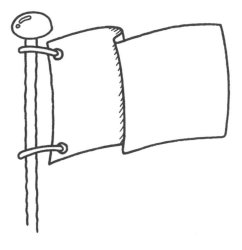

_____

_____

_____

_____

_____

_____

_____

_____

_____

Name: **Date:**

Words for today

flag

flake

flash

float

fly

flying

flashing

you

Learning objective

Phonemes
Consonants: /s/,/t/,/m/,/p,/n/,/d/,
/k/ (as grapheme ck), /ng/,/y/
Vowels: /a/,/ar/,/ae/,/i/,/u/,/or/ (as in *your*)

Target words
stamp, stand, star, start, stay, stuck, sting, your

Teacher's notes

Worksheet 12a

- Photocopy this page and help the child to cut out the target words.

- Help the child blend the phonemes to read the words, taking the opportunity to revise the phonemes. Depending on your school's policy you may wish to encourage the child to repeat both the names of the letters and the sounds they make in each of the words (*stamp, stand, star, start, stay, stuck, sting, your*).

Worksheet 12b

- Ask the child to point to the letters at the top of the page and to tell you the sounds they make.

- Dictate the following words to the child: **stamp, stand, star, start, stay, stuck, sting, your**. You may need to repeat each word several times, making sure that the phonemes are pronounced clearly. Showing the child the words they have cut out then covering them while you dictate them one at a time can be a very effective technique. It is important that the child is fully supported and gains lots of praise where s/he is successful, even with part of a word.

- Ensure that the child has seen each word correctly written before asking him/her to attempt to write the words in the appropriate places in the sentences. The sentences provided include quite complex words and the child will need some support in reading them. Encourage the child to make sense of the sentences so that the task of inserting words is made easier.

- As an additional activity you could make up some oral sentences together using some of the words and pointing at the target words on the sheet as you say them e.g. *Stick a stamp on the letter. If you stand on a bee it may sting your foot.*

- Write down one of the sentences for the child to copy. Encourage him/her to write clearly, following the school's handwriting policy for letter formation, and to start the sentence with a capital letter and to end it with a full stop.

Worksheet 12c

- This sheet includes the seven target words with the consonant cluster **st** in each one together with an extra word, *your*. The extra word is a useful high frequency word and can be used for an 'odd one out' activity.

- This sheet could be copied for display purposes but can also be used to provide the child with extra practice in writing the words. There are three writing lines for each word, enabling the child to use large and smaller writing. You may like to write each word on the first of the two smaller writing lines so that the child can copy your writing in the correct style used by your school.

TARGET WORDS

| stamp | stand | star | start |
| stay | stuck | sting | your |

What sounds do the letters make?

s t a ck st y i ng

Listen to your teacher. Write the words.

_____ _____ _____ _____

_____ _____ _____ _____

Use the correct words to fill the gaps in the sentences.

Can you see a _____ in the sky?

I would like to _____ in a hotel.

Sometimes I get _____ on my maths.

Now write a sentence of your own.

_____

_____

Name: _____ **Date:** _____

Words for today

stamp

stand

star

start

stay

stuck

sting

your

13a

Phonemes
Consonants: /s/,/m/,/k/,/t/,/d/,/p/,/n/,/l/,/f/,/t/
Vowels: /a/ or /ar/ (as in after), /ur/ (as in after),
/e/,/ae/,/i/, /ie/. In this set of words the split digraphs i_e
and a_e are introduced, producing the /ae/ and /ie/ phonemes.

Target words
skim, sky, skate, skid,
skip, skin, skill, after

Teacher's notes

Worksheet 13a

- Photocopy this page, then help the child to cut out the letter tiles.
- Help the child to blend the sounds and arrange the tiles to make words. There are many words that can be made, e.g. *ask* and *disk*. Praise the child for finding these but then encourage him/her to experiment with words that start with the blend **sk**.
- In all of the words in this set, apart from the 'odd one out' word, the phonemes /s/ and /k/ are blended together although they are two distinct sounds. Discuss the two letters and the sounds that they make individually then help the child to say the consonant blend **sk**.

Worksheet 13b

- Dictate the following words: **skim, sky, skate, skid, skip, skin, skill, after**. You may need to repeat each word several times to help the child to segment it into its phonemes so that s/he can write it.
- As an additional activity you could make up some oral sentences together using some of the words and pointing at the target words on the sheet as you say them e.g. *I can skate with great skill. After school I like to skip.*
- Choose two of the sentences for the child to write out. Encourage him/her to write clearly, following the school's handwriting policy for letter formation, and to start the sentence with a capital letter and to end it with a full stop.

Worksheet 13c

- This sheet includes the seven target words with the cluster **sk** at the start of each one together with an extra word, *after*. The extra word is a useful high frequency word and can be used for an 'odd one out' activity.
- This sheet could be copied for display purposes but can also be used to provide the child with extra practice in writing the words. There are three writing lines for each word, enabling the child to use large and smaller writing. You could write each word on the first of the two smaller writing lines so that the child can copy your writing in the correct style used by your school.

LETTER TILES

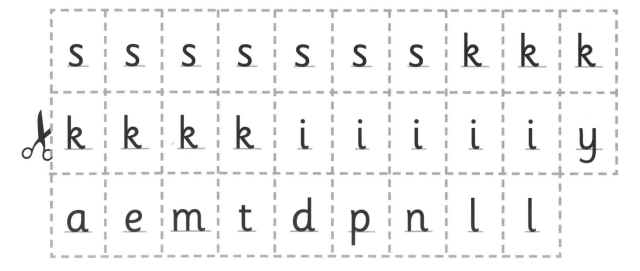

Andrew Brodie: Supporting Phonics & Spelling © A & C Black Publishers Ltd. 2006

Name: _____ **Date:** _____

Listen to your teacher. Write the words.

Write two sentences using one or more of the words.

Andrew Brodie: Supporting Phonics & Spelling © A & C Black Publishers Ltd. 2006

Name:

Date:

Words for today

skim

sky

skate

skid

skip

skin

skill

after

Learning objective

Phonemes	**Target words**
Consonants: /t/,/r/,/n/,/p/,/g/, /k/ (as grapheme ck), /l/ **Vowels:** /ae/,/a/,/i/,/u/,/ie/,/ur/	train, track, trick, truck, try, trap, tray, girl

Teacher's notes

Worksheet 14a

- Photocopy this page and help the child cut out the target words.
- Help the child blend the phonemes to read the words, taking the opportunity to revise the phonemes. Depending on your school's policy you may wish to encourage the child to repeat both the names of the letters and the sounds they make in each of the words (*train, track, trick, truck, try, trap, tray, girl*).
- Can the child hear the sounds in each word? Point out the letters **a** and **i** in the word train. Discuss the sounds that these letters can make when used on their own, then the sound that they make together – **ai** makes the sound /ae/.

Worksheet 14b

- Dictate the following sentences to the child, providing help with words such as tripped and dropped that are not in the list of target words. You may like to take the opportunity to discuss the fact that the consonant **p** is doubled when **ed** is added to trip or drop.

  Trick the fly so you can trap it.
  The girl tripped and dropped the tray.
  A red train came down the track.

- As an additional activity you could make up some oral sentences together using some of the words and pointing at the target words on the sheet as you say them.
- Write down one of the sentences for the child to copy. Encourage him/her to write clearly, following the school's handwriting policy for letter formation, and to start each sentence with a capital letter and to end it with a full stop.

Worksheet 14c

- This sheet includes the seven target words with the consonant cluster **tr** in each one together with an extra word, *girl*. The extra word is a useful high frequency word and can be used for an 'odd one out' activity.
- This sheet could be copied for display purposes but can also be used to provide the child with extra practice in writing the words. There are three writing lines for each word, enabling the child to use large and smaller writing. You could write each word on the first of the two smaller writing lines so that the child can copy your writing in the correct style used by your school.

TARGET WORDS

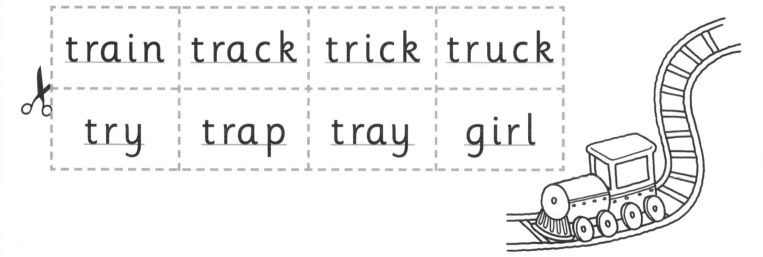

train   track   trick   truck

try   trap   tray   girl

Name: **Date:**

Listen to your teacher. Write the sentences.

Now write a sentence of your own.

Name: **Date:**

Words for today

train

track

trick

truck

try

trap

tray

girl

Andrew Brodie: Supporting Phonics & Spelling © A & C Black Publishers Ltd. 2006

15a

Learning objective

Phonemes
Consonants: /th/,/t/,/r/,/s/,/l/,/ch/,/w/,/sh/, /k/,/n/,/p/
Vowels: /ee/, /o/

Target words
three, tree, sleep, cheek, sweep, sheep, week, one

Teacher's notes

Worksheet 15a

- Photocopy this sheet and help the child cut out the target words.

- Support the child in blending the phonemes to read the words taking the opportunity to revise the phonemes. Depending on your school's policy, you could encourage the child to repeat both the names of the letters and the sounds they make in each of the words.

Worksheet 15b

- Ask the child to point to the letters at the top of the page and to tell you the sounds they make.

- Dictate the words **three, tree, sleep, cheek, sweep, sheep, week, one** to the child. You may need to repeat each word several times, making sure that the phonemes are pronounced clearly. Showing the child the words they have cut out then covering them while you dictate them one at a time can be a very effective technique. It is important that the child is fully supported and gains lots of praise where s/he is successful, even with part of a word.

- Ensure that the child has seen each word correctly written before asking him/her to attempt to write the words in the appropriate places in the sentences. Encourage the child to make sense of the sentences so that the task of inserting words is made easier. One of the sentences provided includes the word *because*. There are many ideas for memorising this word, including 'big elephants can always upset small elephants' – perhaps the child could make up his/her own mnemonic.

- As an additional activity you could make up some oral sentences together using some of the words and pointing at the target words on the sheet as you say them e.g. *I went to sleep in a tree. One day I saw three sheep*.

- Write down one of the sentences for the child to copy. Encourage him/her to write clearly, following the school's handwriting policy for letter formation and to start the sentence with a capital letter and to end it with a full stop.

Worksheet 15c

- This sheet includes the seven target words with the grapheme **ee** in each one, together with an extra word, *one*. The extra word is a useful high frequency word and can be used for an 'odd one out' activity.

- This sheet could be copied for display purposes but can also be used to provide the child with extra practice in writing the words. There are three writing lines for each word, enabling the child to use large and smaller writing. You may like to write each word on the first of the two smaller writing lines so that the child can copy your writing in the correct style used by your school.

TARGET WORDS

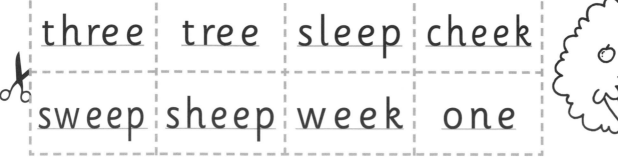

Name: **Date:**

What sounds do the letters make?

th r t sl p ch k sw sh ee

Listen to your teacher. Write the words.

_____   _____   _____   _____

_____   _____   _____   _____

Use the correct words to fill the gaps in the sentences.

Go to _____ because
it's night time.

One, two, _____,
four, five, six.

I had to _____ the
dust away.

Now write a sentence of your own.

_____

_____

Name: _____ **Date:** _____

Words for today

three _____ _____

tree _____ _____

sleep _____ _____

cheek _____ _____

sweep _____ _____

sheep _____ _____

week _____ _____

one _____ _____

16a

Learning objective

Phonemes

Consonants: /l/ (as grapheme ll), /b/,/w/,
/s/,/t/,/f/,/h/,/k/ (as grapheme c), /m/

Vowel: /or/

Target words
ball, wall, stall, fall, hall, call, small, saw

Teacher's notes

Worksheet 16a

- Photocopy this page, then help the child to cut out the letter tiles.

- Revise the phonemes with the child. In most of the words in this set the phoneme /l/ is created through the use of double **l** and the phoneme /or/ is created through the use of letter **a** (except in the 'odd one out' word where the same phoneme is represented by the grapheme aw.)

- When you feel the child is confident with the phonemes, help him/her to blend the sounds and arrange the letter tiles to make words.

Worksheet 16b

- Dictate the words **ball, wall, stall, fall, hall, call, small, saw** one at a time. You may need to repeat each word several times to help the child segment it into its phonemes so that s/he can write it.

- As an additional activity you could make up some oral sentences together using some of the words and pointing at the target words on the sheet as you say them e.g. *I hit the ball against the wall of the hall. I saw a small boy fall.*

- Write down one of the sentences for the child to copy. Encourage him/her to write clearly, following the school's handwriting policy for letter formation, and to start the sentence with a capital letter and to end it with a full stop.

Worksheet 16c

- The sheet includes the seven target words with the grapheme **ll** at the end of each one, together with an extra word, *saw*. The extra word is a useful high frequency word and can be used for an 'odd one out' activity.

- This sheet could be copied for display purposes but can also be used to provide the child with extra practice in writing the words. There are three writing lines for each word, enabling the child to use large and smaller writing. You may like to write each word on the first of the two smaller writing lines so that the child can copy your writing in the correct style used by your school.

LETTER TILES

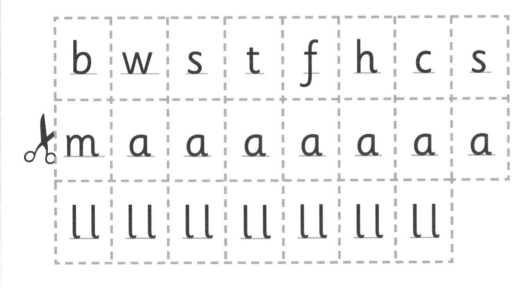

Name: **Date:**

Listen to your teacher. Write the words.

Now write a sentence of your own.

Andrew Brodie: Supporting Phonics & Spelling © A & C Black Publishers Ltd. 2006

Name: _____   **Date:** _____

Words for today

ball   _____   _____

wall   _____   _____

stall   _____   _____

fall   _____   _____

hall   _____   _____

call   _____   _____

small   _____   _____

saw   _____   _____

 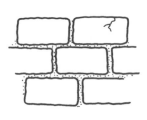   

Learning objective

Phonemes

Consonants: /f/ (as grapheme ff), /k/ (as graphemes k and c), /l/,/s/,/t/,/n/,/h/,/m/

Vowels: /o/,/i/,/u/,/ae/ (as split digraph a_e)

Target words

off, cliff, fluff, stuff, sniff, huff, stiff, make

Teacher's notes

Worksheet 17a

- Photocopy this page and help the child cut out the target words.

- Support the child in blending the phonemes to read the words, taking the opportunity to revise the phonemes. Depending on your school's policy you may wish to encourage the child to repeat both the names of the letters and the sounds they make in each of the words.

- Read each word to the child, then ask him/her to read each one back to you. Can the child hear the sounds in each word? Look at some of the blends, **cl**, **fl**, **st**, **sn** and discuss the way the letters work together in these. Point out the letter **a** and the final **e** in the 'odd one out' word *make*. Discuss the sounds that these letters can make when used on their own, then the sound that they make when used together in the split digraph **a_e**. This makes the sound /ae/. The final **e** is separated from the **a** by a single consonant and 'makes the **a** say its name'.

Worksheet 17b

- Dictate the following sentences to the child, providing support with words such as *bird, flew, don't* and *mistake* that are not in the list of target words, by segmenting each word into its phonemes. Note that the word *mistake* includes the same split digraph as the word *make*.

  The bird flew off the top of the cliff.
  Don't get in a huff if you make a mistake.
  My legs get stiff if I run for a long time.

- As an additional activity you could make up some oral sentences together using some of the words and pointing at the focus words on the sheet as you say them

- You could write one of the sentences for the child to copy. Encourage him/her to write clearly, following the school's handwriting policy for letter formation, and to start each sentence with a capital letter and to end it with a full stop.

Worksheet 17c

- This sheet includes the seven target words with the grapheme **ff** in each one together with an extra word, *make*. The extra word is a useful high frequency word and can be used for an 'odd one out' activity.

- This sheet could be copied for display purposes but can also be used to provide the child with extra practice in writing the words. There are three writing lines for each word, enabling the child to use large and smaller writing. You may like to write each word on the first of the two smaller writing lines so that the child can copy your writing in the correct style used by your school.

TARGET WORDS

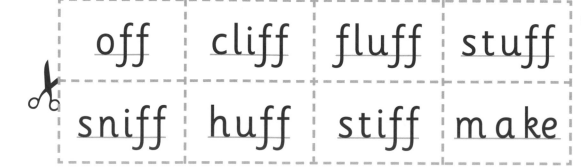

off   cliff   fluff   stuff

sniff   huff   stiff   make

Andrew Brodie: Supporting Phonics & Spelling © A & C Black Publishers Ltd. 2006

Name:

Date:

Listen to your teacher. Write the sentences.

Now write a sentence of your own.

Name: **Date:**

Words for today

off

cliff

fluff

stuff

sniff

huff

stiff

make

Andrew Brodie: Supporting Phonics & Spelling © A & C Black Publishers Ltd. 2006

Learning objective

Phonemes
Consonants: /d/, /r/, /n/, /s/, /m/, /l/, /p/, /n/.
Vowels: /ae/, /e/, /u/, /ie/ (as grapheme y),
/ee/(as grapheme ea), /i/, /o/, /ew/.

Target words
drain, dress, drum, dry,
dream, drill, drop, new

Teacher's notes

Worksheet 18a

- Photocopy this page and help the child to cut out the target words.

- Support the child in blending the phonemes to read the words, taking the opportunity to revise the phonemes. Depending on your school's policy you may wish to encourage the child to repeat both the names of the letters and the sounds they make in each of the words.

Worksheet 18b

- Ask the child to point to the letters at the top of the page and to tell you the sounds they make.

- Dictate the words **drain, dress, drum, dry, dream, drill, drop, new** to the child, helping him/her to segment each word into its phonemes so that s/he can choose the correct letters to spell the words. You may need to repeat each word several times, making sure that the phonemes are pronounced clearly.

- Ensure that the child can see each word correctly written before asking him/her to attempt to write the words in the appropriate places in the sentences. Encourage the child to make sense of the sentences so that the task of inserting words is made easier.

- As an additional activity you or the child could make up some extra sentences using some of the words and pointing at the focus words on the sheet as you say them e.g. *Don't drop the drill. I dry myself after my shower.*

- You could write down one of the sentences for the child to copy. Encourage him/her to write clearly, following the school's handwriting policy for letter formation, and to start the sentence with a capital letter and to end it with a full stop.

Worksheet 18c

- This sheet includes the seven target words with the consonant cluster **dr** in each one together with an extra word, *one*. The extra word is a useful high frequency word and can be used for an 'odd one out' activity.

- This sheet could be copied for display purposes but can also be used to provide the child with extra practice in writing the words. There are three writing lines for each word, enabling the child to use large and smaller writing. You could write each word on the first of the two smaller writing lines so that the child can copy your writing in the correct style used by your school.

TARGET WORDS

drain	dress	drum	dry
dream	drill	drop	new

Name: **Date:**

What sounds do the letters make?

d r e u y i o ai
ss ea ew dr

Listen to your teacher. Write the words.

_____ _____ _____ _____

_____ _____ _____ _____

Use the correct words to fill the gaps in the sentences.

The baby had a new _____ then she got it in a mess.

A _____ of water went down the _____.

Last night I had an amazing _____.

Now write a sentence of your own.

_____

_____

Andrew Brodie: Supporting Phonics & Spelling © A & C Black Publishers Ltd. 2006

Name: _____   **Date:** _____

Words for today

drain   _____   _____

dress   _____   _____

drum   _____   _____

dry   _____   _____

dream   _____   _____

drill   _____   _____

drop   _____   _____

new

19a ★

Phonemes
Consonants: /p/,/r/,/m/,/n/,/t/,/d/,/s/,/z/
Vowels: /ae/ (as grapheme ay), /a/,/i/,/o/,/e/,
/ie/ (as split digraph i_e)

Target words
pray, pram, print, prod,
press, price, prize, time

Teacher's notes

Worksheet 19a

- Photocopy this page and help the child cut out the target words.

- Support the child in blending the phonemes to read the words, taking the opportunity to revise the phonemes. Depending on your school's policy you may wish to encourage the child to repeat both the names of the letters and the sounds they make in each of the words.

- Can the child hear the sounds in each word? Look at the blend **pr** and discuss the way the letters work together in this. Point out the letter **i** and the final **e** in the words *price* and *prize* and in the 'odd one out' word *time*. Discuss the sounds that these letters can make when used on their own, then the sound that they make when used together in the split digraph: **i_e** makes the sound /ie/. In each of these three words the final **e** is separated from the **i** by a single consonant and 'makes the **i** say its name'.

Worksheet 19b

- Dictate the following sentences to the child, providing support with words such as *baby*, *won*, *first* and *book* that are not in the list of target words by encouraging the child to segment the words into their phonemes.

  The baby in the pram won first prize.
  What price is this book?
  Is it time for bed yet?

- Discuss the fact that the last two of these sentences are questions and will need question marks at the end instead of full stops.

- As an additional activity you or the child could make up some extra sentences using some of the words and pointing at the target words on the sheet as you say them.

- You could write one of the sentences for the child to copy. Encourage him/her to write clearly, following the school's handwriting policy for letter formation, and to start each sentence with a capital letter and to end it with a full stop or with a question mark if appropriate.

Worksheet 19c

- This sheet includes the seven target words with the blend **pr** at the start of each one together with an extra word, *time*. The extra word is a useful high frequency word and can be used for an 'odd one out' activity.

- This sheet could be copied for display purposes but can also be used to provide the child with extra practice in writing the words. There are three writing lines for each word, enabling the child to use large and smaller writing. You may like to write each word on the first of the two smaller writing lines so that the child can copy your writing in the correct style used by your school.

TARGET WORDS

pray	pram	print	prod
press	price	prize	time

Andrew Brodie: Supporting Phonics & Spelling © A & C Black Publishers Ltd. 2006

19b **Name:** **Date:**

Listen to your teacher. Write the sentences.

_____

_____

_____

_____

_____

_____

_____

_____

_____

Now write a sentence of your own.

_____

_____

Name: **Date:**

Words for today

pray

pram

print

prod

press

price

prize

time

   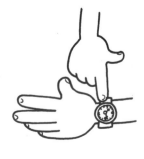